GIRL'S GUIDE TO LEAVING

WISCONSIN POETRY SERIES

Edited by Ronald Wallace and Sean Bishop

GIRL'S GUIDE TO LEAVING

LAURA VILLAREAL

The University of Wisconsin Press

Publication of this book has been made possible, in part, through support from the Brittingham Trust.

The University of Wisconsin Press
728 State Street, Suite 443
Madison, Wisconsin 53706
uwpress.wisc.edu

Gray's Inn House, 127 Clerkenwell Road
London EC1R 5DB, United Kingdom
eurospanbookstore.com

Printed in the United States of America
This book may be available in a digital edition.

Library of Congress Cataloging-in-Publication Data

Names: Villareal, Laura, 1992- author.
Title: Girl's guide to leaving / Laura Villareal.
Other titles: Wisconsin poetry series.
Description: Madison, Wisconsin : The University of Wisconsin Press, [2022]
  | Series: Wisconsin poetry series
Identifiers: LCCN 2021038185 | ISBN 9780299336844 (paperback)
Subjects: LCGFT: Poetry.
Classification: LCC PS3622.I49397 G57 2022 | DDC 811/.6—dc23
LC record available at https://lccn.loc.gov/2021038185>

For my mom & her mother, their dichos

CONTENTS

GIRL'S GUIDE TO LEAVING

GIRL'S GUIDE TO LEAVING

in the beginning there were white owls with the faces of women
the ones your grandmother warned you about
the ones your mother said were only Mexican folklore
but now you see them everywhere

as you drive late at night on a road
that turns sharply like a windup toy,
reminding you it doesn't belong to you & never will

you know the remedy: hug
the curves until they croon for you
like your grandmother's music boxes

you've always known how to charm
a place into loving you back
but for now—this state, this road, & even the sky
don't belong to you

your want sparks
a miracle of white feathers

your want cores you
awake each morning

you come from a long line of wandering men—
men who cut night in half
just to leave a city
with an infant cooing in her sleep

in the beginning women sold their hearts
for freedom & were vilified in legends
you're the first girl in your family
to never stop moving
your legend is that you write your own legend

heartless girl, if you don't keep moving
any place could become a cage

& you've already escaped once
luck doesn't occur twice, you know

TRAPPING SEASON

Within the thick evergreens, there's a snow-bearded cottage blowing smoke from its pipe. The cottage has makeshift patches on its elbows, coffee-stained windows, & stories to tell. A man stokes the fire—cracks wood into sparks at the hearth. He puts out food for the foxes. A vixen eats it without knowing she must give something in return.

He pushed me against the wood-paneled wall, restrained my arms. Rigid breath in my ear, "I love you . . ." If my wrist bones shattered, I'd be able to slip away. ". . . if you leave me, I'll kill myself." Crying. A glass man fell to the floor. If I left right then, would his blood be liquid or sand? It's unclear how to leave when his body guards the door.

The vixen now sleeps at the hearth. Heat radiates in every follicle of her fur. Never does she go without a meal. She's glassblowing a man's heart, precariously spinning molten sand.

I don't know who taught me to pull a knife from a chest—a reflecting pool blade ebbing slow blood. Not sure who taught me words to coax a knife from his hands. Not sure anyone would believe me if I told them.

As the flames slumber under the charcoal skin of their logs, the vixen continues to dream. The floorboards groan under the weight of footfalls, which startles her awake. She inhales too deeply, rousing the embers. An axe crashes to the floor.

No one ever hears when she scratches at the windows or howls. No one hears the vixen except the ancient house. It has stories to tell, but no one ever said it would repeat them. Snow falls off the eaves. Needles fall off the trees. The vixen's tail hangs from the ceiling.

People ask about the bruises & I tell them I'm clumsy. I tell them they're purple pansies, yellow-eyed I love yous winding their green stems around my body. The truth gets caught in my throat.

THE CONDITIONS FOR EXISTING AS PROPOSED BY X, Y, & Z

(WHAT MAKES SENSE, WHAT'S SAFE, WHAT'S PRODUCTIVE)

After JR Mahung

X.	Y.	Z.
I think	every question is rhetorical	my eyes dodge my own gaze
to enact violence on another person	my answer eats its way up	until I can confess
I enact violence on myself		like a vine around a fence
& I admit violence hums back	I wait for amends	all answers get strangled
over my body laced in grief	knowing nothing can ever fill	knowing they've been lost on the way
ripening into	a needful bruise	a lifetime as an overflow
I have to save myself	before it's too late	

BEFORE SKIPPING TOWN

the last light casting your shadow should be neon
red of a Texaco star, sidle up to your '56 Eldorado.

the gas station attendant won't remember you,
but he'll remember the nautilus

tattoo on your ankle—so out of place
in the desert. you leave your skeleton

milkweed at home & trade up,
maybe for some gravel ghost

as white as a cigarette wish.
you imagine there's stolen money

filling an attaché case in your truck
instead of crumpled cans. all sharp edges

glimmer like spinning wheels to prick your finger.
but out in the scrub brush there are no fairy-tale endings,

only legends of women pleading into the night air.

SARDINE SPINE

Never have I seen vertebrae so small,
so white like a strand of pearls
without luster, unclasped.
The spine is tenuous,

made for a touch more
tender than mine—

The sardine smells like the holes
of my pierced ears.
My body has never learned to heal

even after all this time. I keep pushing
metal posts through my ears so they'll stay
open. But maybe I should let them close.

My body is as stubborn as I am,
but which of us knows best?

Maybe if I could hold the sardine's spine
gently, without breaking it,
it would become a pearl necklace clasped
to my throat as I speak the answer.

THE LONG TRAJECTORY OF GRIEF

A squeal cracks bright like hot metal in water. Before
the sun has licked across the fields, I wonder how to save myself

before guilt sets like a stain. I wonder
if the constellations above me can lift shame or if they're only

a temporary solution for what I feel. In the morning
I find 3 wild boars in the street, dead. A red

bumper lying near one of their carcasses.
Is the nature of a crash to always leave something behind?

Fog glimmers up from the road forsaken
by first light. I pretend not to notice

your absence—how my car isn't spiced with your oakmoss
& mint anymore. But I pray the vultures pick me

clean like a Tibetan sky
burial before anyone smells grief on me.

AFTERWARDS

After Miguel Hernández

for years my ruling planet was grief
I traveled through life engulfed

              anyone who touched me blistered
              but I couldn't see who added kindling

when I wanted to speak the truth,   buckshot fell from my mouth &
it only rose when I was a wasteland   my words burned for entire months

I wanted to scream when I saw   anyone who had your face
an open field full of shotguns   locked me in a memory

some years I was more animal than   severed root
burning star unable to satiate   revisiting the source of

longing to unknot the past   bruises that were no longer
only able to hide inside   purple & yellow galaxies

the mud nest of my body   kept beating a lullaby
where at least birds would rest   after the gun was lowered

I STILL CHECK FOR MONSTERS BEFORE I GO TO BED

When the night bloggers have
had their fill of memes & trending acts of
violence, I search for you:
[URL redacted]
I want to know how
you're doing. Well,
I want to know that you're un-
happy, that you're 2,000 miles away,
& you can't touch me. In my dreams,
you appear disguised as
a shoebox on my doorstep.
When I open you,
there's shotgun & flare
gun shells. The too familiar
odor of Diesel
cologne, brass & birdshot—
it still makes me want to run,
but I don't, because I see
a girl sitting in all the chaos
tweeting in Morse code:
3 dots, 3 dashes, 3 dots.
You'll awaken & transform
when I try to rescue her,
but I have a plan. I'll wake myself up
just enough to control my dream—
to turn myself into glass
before you hit me. This time,
it'll be your blood instead of mine.

BABY TEETH

some afternoons music sways like a broken screen door
in a distant part of a house I was never a god in. it's flooded

with marigold light & it makes sense that my milk
teeth have been traded to deep south spiritualists.

they say I was born fanged & feathered like
no child from heaven should be. a miracle

that when I lost those teeth I became human.
my feathers burned one by one each year of my life.

I'm tired of the way my mouth fills with guava
seeds like infant pearls after. give me blood

from pomegranates. I demand tears
in every screen door in the south until

they fall off their hinges or every onyx tooth
is planted in the ground around my body. wait.

let a song come first from a black storm rolling
over the still sorghum fields. I am nothing

if not determined to re-create myself as a god.
so let the birds steal my teeth from the ground

& hide them in their babies' open beaks.
listen for the heavy stillness before the rain

& know I am waiting to become whole again.

OUTGROWING A HOME

Tell us again about La Llorona.
Mimic her weeping, "Mis hijos . . .
Mis hijos! ¿Dónde están mis hijos?"

I switch off the light to see
fish shoaling across the bedroom walls.

Those nights I never dreamed
of leaving. Everything I wanted fit

in the nail of my pinky—
yearning only 2 centimeters wide.

These days I lie
awake. Everything I want has outgrown my body
& radiates into the endless fields

outside my house. Yearning diffuses
2 centimeters more each day.

As I leave, I can hear
my house calling out to me:

"Mi hija. ¿Dónde está mi hija?"

DESERT NOTE

on survival I know only this when land is inhospitable
you must uproot entirely tumble until you find better
land to put down roots listen this part is important
you must never let yourself try & find the first place
you took root you must live like a tumbleweed
you must never call out into the desert blue night
but you will anyways I know this you'll cry out
as the coyotes do weep like cacti beg the wind to
take you back & you'll survive when no answer comes

THE ASTRONOMER'S DAUGHTER

I haven't seen the stars since August,
but I remember each pinhole of light.

Silver coyote teeth
marks on astral deerskin. In the distance,
whimpers & howls.

I haven't seen the stars since August,
but seldom think of running with coyotes

or chasing the full moon until it's new again.
Except when I chart constellations

on the body of a man or woman,
the restlessness becomes unbearable.
But I like it that way.

When I disappear, I only leave teeth
marks. I can hear whimpers
& howls in the distance.

I like it that way.

CRUSH

I find a rattlesnake in the morning
    coiled on my porch, rattle raised & shaking
& remember last night.

M messaged asking how long a crush lasted.
I forgot to answer

            her question before asking,
When I moved, did I take all our stories with me?

She didn't reply,
but American Football's "Never Meant"
is the first song on a playlist she made me.

My mom used to tell me
    everything dangerous sounds
like something familiar.

Even a tornado
reminds me of trains passing at night
    behind my grandmother's house.

Even a crush is a rattlesnake, tail
    deep in its own gullet.

Most people don't know the snake's rattle
    sounds like flowing water
from a garden hose
            until they're bit.

HOME IS WHERE THE CLOSET IS

Home is where I put my whole self away
    in the garage or the attic or inside
        a part of me I won't visit soon.

My identity knots around everyone else's finger in Texas.
    I forgot I was brown
        until Texas pointed to the border.

I forgot my orientation was straight
    to hell if I love another woman.
        I'm having trouble adjusting

the light so I look straight enough not to get fired.
    I whisper the word *queer*
        over & over like a spell—

to remind myself I'll come back for it again later
    in a new city, with a new job,
        when there's enough money to be alive.

Most days I want to grieve
    & I want all the stars to grieve with me
        because in Texas even the moon hides

herself behind the clouds—
    away from every woman she loves.

INSIDE THE FOXHOLE

My features are small,
expressionless. My lovers say
I look like a doll. Today
I climbed into a black dollhouse
& felt more at home than anywhere
I've ever been. The wild in me
stopped howling, stopped pulsing
through my legs. Egyptians used mirrors
to reflect light into dark spaces.
As I walk to my apartment, the buildings fill
dim streets with the last segment of sunlight.
I begin thinking of how the wetness
between my legs might spill out
of my black lace panties & fill the gutter
with quicksilver. The Gibbous Moon above
Newark Penn Station watches me.
I wait for her to call me, to say,
Hide where I can't find you.
She hasn't called me by name
since I walked home
with runs in my stockings.
I heard her voice on the wind
once say: *If we believed in God,*
we'd both be damned. I told her
I liked soft violence best,
like a starling fallen into a foxhole.
But didn't tell her I cried
during a dream I had

of holding my melting planet.
Above me, a plane flies
across the tangerine sky
leaving a contrail. Instead of one long, perfect
white streak, it comes out in Braille.
The contrail reads: *Never have I been so alone.*
With no way of feeling those words,
I walk more quickly. In my apartment,
I striptease for the woman I'm seeing.
She pushes me on my bed.
Her hands are cold. She licks quicksilver
from between my legs. Stops.
Says she can taste the champagne I drank—
can hear giddy bubbles filling each
& every one of my moans. Sometimes I want
to say: *If only your body was a home,*
if only I wasn't hollow like a doll.

INSIDE ALL THE PLACES I CAN'T SEE

When I turn on the garbage disposal,
its guttural groaning makes me want
to put my hand down the black-lipped drain,
to be certain that pain exists
even inside a place I can't see.

DOWN BY THE WATER

Battery Park, October 2015

I unspool the evening   by myself

near the water back home
nothing changes
the river remains warm

all year long I feel mercurial
like honey locust or   a winged beast

I wait & wait
& learn to tie knots from grass-

hopper legs,   marking minutes
night scrapes by slow—hard

enough that I hear it leaving
silver splinters behind   I never stop looking for

a new place to rebuild myself
I'm so far away from   home

I no longer hear cicadas
swarm inside my body

but some mornings   I wake up
with golden shells
wreathed in my hair

23

SLASH AND BURN

A stranger's hothouse grows my heart

at 3 a.m. I'm leaving,

unhurried, like first kindling

nestled into a field's edge.

The devil's hour spills ash, muddied & familiar.

Even the guard dogs continue sleeping

as the latch clicks into the strike plate,

as I run a stick across the fence line

so it sounds like footfalls of someone

chasing behind me. Not even a block away,

I make Persephone's mistake.

I knew I would

after she asked me to stay &

cultivate my gods.

But something still runs wild in me.

A stranger's hothouse has harvested

my heart. Climbing into bed

next to her, I continue insisting

I didn't scorch the earth

to make room for her & an ember

blossoms as simply a morning lily.

IF I INVITED YOU TO LOVE ME

I'd tell you I'm a 4-way intersection
in a town made for shooting movies
& yes, the traffic light still works.

I'd tell you my burial ground planted a home
& everything I own fits in my tear ducts.

I'd tell you even after long-term collapse
black holes go undetected.

I'd tell you my Netflix queue is trash
because some nights elongate
& I trick myself into thinking
a romcom will bore me to sleep
but I watch the whole damn movie
until, crying, I fall asleep
every. single. time.

I'd tell you I don't think ideal love
looks anything like a romcom.

I'd tell you most people don't know
rollie pollies are crustaceans
& ask what else people misidentify.

I'd tell you I've gone to museums 52 times this year,
but I only go when I'm lonely.

I'd tell you I'm not always sure
being alone is worse than
allowing someone to splinter me.

I'd tell you I've never
seen a relationship that wasn't barter
or been in one that wasn't outright robbery,
but vicarious living isn't enough anymore.

MOTHER // MONSTER

At dinner, my dad says after I was born
   I devoured laced milk. My mother's
      brined sorrow was my first elixir for sleep.

I learned from her how to cry without stopping
   in those first months.

Motherhood
   & its sorrow were entwined monsters.
      Let him speak plainly, he would have left her

alone with my monstrous infancy & my brother,
   only 3, playing with his trains on the floor.

I want to reduce berry down to bitter.
   I want to tell stories of my self-centeredness like I invented it.

The trick is to tell stories like a man.
      The trick is every story is a hero's journey
  if it's told without remorse.

My inheritance is my mother's honeycombed sorrow,
   my father's deluged retreat.

I read once that female babies survive stressful pregnancies
      more often than males.
Even at birth they leave when it's too hard.

Misread:
   "mothers" as monster,

       miss the other in the middle, moth
drawn to bright window at night

as he leaves, & says the children are only hers.

THANKSGIVINGS

San Marcos, Texas

Around noon the sheriff pulled up to my aunt's house.
My cousins had been shooting guns
around back. Bullets fell like ash in the neighbor's yard.

My mom told me to stay inside. I didn't
understand how anyone could hang a Confederate flag

in their living room. I sat on cowhide
underneath a pair of antlers & tried to understand

keeping the dead as trophies. I was 9.
My skin was the same color of deer pelt. Not bone white

like my cousins'. I wandered the property by myself.
As I wandered, I found bones shattered

among the wildflowers. I leapt back,
got caught on the fence.
Cacti grew near the barbed wire, without blooming.

Like Pappy, I was disinclined to speaking.
He only spoke to remind my aunts & uncles,

We didn't cross the border, the border crossed us.
By this he meant, *Like cacti*
we only thrive because of our shallow roots.

San Antonio, Texas

I remember teeth in the pozole.
Smoke clouded like carnations
from my uncles' Marlboros.

My mom said it was hominy, not teeth. My imagination
outgrew my body in this house.

Monet & Renoir filled the walls in the den.
No cousins here at least.
Everyone looked like me & Grandma

had an out-of-tune piano I loved.
I played "Ode to Joy" until Pete, her dog, howled.
She always told me to stop

feeding the stray cats
under her rose bushes. My brother played
Gameboy on her ivy-green couch. After dinner,

I wound all the music boxes
& sat outside watching the sun burn
the skyline into vine charcoal silhouettes.

HEART ATTACK

After I tell my mom I have the feeling of sand falling
inside the veins of my left arm,

she checks to see if I'm still breathing in my sleep—
holds a mirror to my nose to see
if a cloud will smile back in the starlit reflection.

> She worries
> my heart will answer whether sound comes
> when a tree falls in the woods. She worries

the way only a mother
or unreachable dark parts of the ocean do.

We don't talk about hereditary illness
like heart problems, but she knows
> violence skips a generation.

My grandmother's heart was worn
into a wooden hollow, until it echoed
loud enough to quiet the beating.

> I don't tell her motherhood
> is my biggest fear—
> that I can't imagine

the moment before
pulling the mirror away
my face blurry
with a child's breath.

CURAS & DICHOS

My mom tried to reclaim me in small ways, like teaching me cumbia. When I was young, she used to lean in after spinning me to say: *El borracho will lean in too close, breathing his hot alcohol on your neck, that's when you know it's time to leave.* But my hips remain rigid, both native & colonist. My dad's mixed blood is my mixed blood & some part of me knows I'll never be able to steal or own a world.

Even in college, a white woman tried to teach me to dance. She insisted, *I can teach you. All Mexicans can dance—it's in your blood.* She gave up when my hips wouldn't give rhythm, leaving me with her purse & drink at the bar. I didn't tell her about the hooves on her dance partner, sulfur clouding in the air around them. I remember a dicho my mom tells me before I go out, *El diablo nunca duerme—* the trouble I'm looking for will always find me first.

As a small child, my grandmother & mom tried to teach me Spanish using incentives. Showing me chocolate coins, they asked, *¿Qué es esto?* I replied full of child certainty, *Chocolates. Tesoros pequeños.* I'm not comfortable speaking Spanish. Not like my mom & my grandmother at the kitchen table when they try to keep me from eavesdropping. Spanish for serious matters, English for ordinary gossip. *Las pequeñas jarras tienen orejas grandes*, my grandmother used to say about me. As I grew, they spoke faster so I wouldn't keep up. Listening but never speaking, my family says my eyes talk more than I do. Language has always stumbled drunk from my mouth so I loop it around my tongue & hold it until it melts like pocketed gold.

I was 6 when I asked for a Selena doll. It was Christmas & my parents weren't even sure it existed. But they found one & for the first time I saw myself reflected back in a doll. I get regularly asked, *What are you?* Like the other day in Tokyo Mart when a man asked me to translate a package written in Japanese. I told him I didn't know. He asked what I was, but before I could respond, he told me I'm "pretty for a Mexican." People see what they want when they look at me, most search for kinship & think they find it in the wave of my hair, my almond-shaped eyes, or my olive skin. I look for myself in other people too, but only find their questions.

My mom's remedies have always been the same. Boiled cinnamon sticks for empacho. Caldo & VapoRub for everything else. But a week ago, after my brother hydroplaned & crashed his car in a storm, she gave him a spoon of sugar & called it cura de susto. I asked why she'd never given either of us that before. She told me we had

never been close enough to steal marigolds from
Death. I want to ask if she has a cure for longing
to fit in any world. I want to ask if she has a blood
cure for wanting to own what isn't mine. I want
to tell her, but En boca cerrada no entran moscas
is our family motto.

MY WORRIES HAVE WORRIES

so I built little matchstick houses
with large ceilings, a garden for them to grow

tomatoes, cilantro, & carrots
their worry babies will eat

but they chew on the henbit of me anyway
both my past & future entwined into disasters

I tell them I worry about their health
that they're not eating properly

I mother them
the way I do anyone I love

they ask if I love myself
I tug the sleeves of my sweater

begin thatching a leaking roof
water their garden
at night

I can hear them
dancing around a bonfire

all I've built burned
down, a soot snowfall

tomorrow they'll wait for me
& I'll reconstruct their home
anyone would do the same

UNCERTAINTY WITH FISH SCALES

Maybe the boy sifting pebbles by the lakeshore
makes it back home with a guppy in each hand.

Maybe I don't call out his name
& hear fish scales against a dull knife.

Maybe I don't call him mijo or child I'll never want
& maybe I won't mean child I won't know
I want until it's too late.

Maybe I remember tragedy is the easy ending.

Maybe the search party finds him cold,
unharmed in a cave saying he followed duendes
in little green cloaks, heart-shaped

like the elephant ears growing
in my garden
near the barren pond.

Maybe he tells his story with certainty
that the search party is looking for me
like they looked for him.

Maybe the guppies don't gasp lipped o's on the stone god shore.
Maybe they escape the boy's clumsy fingers
& their story begins.

Doesn't every story start with a near miss?

Maybe the boy, the guppies, & I sink lower into the lake
& the lake isn't a lake at all. Maybe it's always been the shore
covered in a trove of lapis lazuli fish scales.

I've said it before, but nothing unmothered ever leaves
without a wake & ripple
like stones crossing the water.

SOLAR ECLIPSE // MYSELF IN ORBIT

Kyle, TX | December 24, 1997

The moon got lost, he said. My brother was 2 years old when he saw his first eclipse. It was July 11, 1991, in Ruiz, Mexico. I was still a distant possibility, but my dad tells this story as we look at slides in my aunt's living room. Each wall has a celestial tapestry, the knowing smirk on the moon & sun's faces, push-pinned to the wall. Smoke wisps past a screen caught in the light of the projector. Back then all my aunts & uncles went to church & their cigarettes burned faster than incense. We all believed God would save us from ourselves.

Home | Childhood

My brother's first word was "clock." Even as a child he was in tune with time's influence on everything. Somehow he's able to tap into the universe's ebb & flow. He loses track of time easily. Forgets what day or month it is, but if asked to let you know when 10 minutes have passed, he doesn't need a clock to do it.

My first word was "food." My lack of depth embarrasses me. As a child, I worked hard to be good at something so I read as many books as I could & memorized vocabulary words. I wanted to be extraordinary like my genius brother. To be smart without even trying.

His IQ is over 140, but he's dyslexic. The kids at school bully him. I don't treat him as well as I should either. I'm mean with envy.

San Antonio, TX | 2001–2006

I'm in the classes for "dumb" kids because I'm not good at math. At my school you're only allowed to be good at both reading & math to be "smart." My reading PSAT scores are in the 95th percentile in the country. I'm given an award with kids from the "smart" classes at a ceremony. A parent asks me what I'm doing there. I don't answer.

I write a letter asking to be in the honors teacher's English class. She lets me take her class after I explain I've read the most books in the school for Accelerated Reading 2 years in a row. In class, I'm quick to answer & understand the high school-level books. I feel like I'm really in the class I should be. Finally.

We write children's stories as a project. My teacher tells me, *I thought you plagiarized your story. I asked my friend in publishing if you did. Did you write that story on your own?*

Kyle, TX | April 4, 1999

My cousins are chasing a chicken with a 5-dollar bill taped to its wing around the yard. I feel self-conscious but play along knowing I'll never catch the golden hen. She flies onto the round hay bale & my cousins start climbing up, unspooling the hay until it's a pile on the lawn. The hen gets away.

My grandfather, Pappy, sits on the porch in his chair, a cigar tucked into his shirt pocket. A trucker hat covers his balding head & dark shaded glasses obscure his eyes.

My skin is as dark as his. I stand out compared to my cousins & my grandmother. They have fair skin that burns quickly in the sun. I want their blue eyes for myself. If I had blue or green eyes, I'd be beautiful like they say on TV. Every part of me feels too big. I wear oversized shirts that swallow my body in totality.

San Antonio, TX | August 2006

I straighten the curl out of my hair & get frustrated when humidity curls it again. I'm not pretty enough to dress girly. My friends tell me I'm one of the boys. They like that I listen to "good" music. Unobtrusive with my band tees, a penumbra of black eyeliner. I reap the benefits of male privilege. I don't realize I'm part of the problem, part of what makes me feel like my body is an unfit home.

San Antonio, TX | 2009-2010

Grief has made me smaller. People notice & comment. My Spanish teacher tells me it must be love that made me skinnier. But it's fear of the next outburst, my parent's relationship becoming a chasm, hospital food by my grandmother's bedside—grief above all else. My PE coach is impressed that I can run faster than I ever could before. He thinks it's because I'm 25 pounds lighter than I was when I started school 3 years ago. I don't tell him I've had practice running away. It's all I ever seem to do nowadays.

Newark, NJ | 2015

My hair is longer than it's ever been, almost long enough for me to donate. All my energy goes into supporting the people I love. Another friend died the summer before. I notice the fullness of my hips in the mirror & like it. No one comments on my weight. I don't own a scale for once in my life.

Each year I love myself more, but doubt returns on the moon's cycle.

Dawson Springs, KY | September 21, 2017

We hear gunshots in the distance. *Who tries to shoot the moon? Who tries to stop an eclipse?* My brother is watching the eclipse silently through a telescope. I feel anxious like the world may be ending & we don't know it yet. Crickets begin their symphony in the yard as the world gets cold. The sunlight turns indigo & everything looks like it's being seen through an Instagram filter.

As the sun comes back up, the rooster crows as if it's a new day. We turn from memory to daylight.

I'm waiting for my own solar eclipse—
waiting to be the main event for even a few minutes.

San Marcos, TX | April 8, 2019

The next major solar eclipse in North America will occur in 5 years. It'll be one of the longest in history. I'll be 31, which is older than I thought I'd live. Even being 26 now feels miraculous. 31-year-old me will ask, *How have I lived this long waiting in the shadow of other people?* I'll bask in a moon without light.

(MY)THOLOGY

my birth was a blank star chart   midday   & minor miracle
    I grew in a cardboard kingdom   built my quiet

harvesting words   for a fallow season   savored them
    like sea glass   left in my pocket   I'd need them later

in my teen years   I battled someone else's monsters
    my own monster was patient   caught in my throat   silence like a wishbone

I broke off the bigger end   born perpetually lucky   or so the story goes
    the monsters left their teeth   burrowed in my body

those hidden treasures   took root in my blood   & luck followed me
    into the dark   picked my bones   into tuning forks   but that was all

I sold my own heart   with a sign that said: *haunted*   *free or best offer*
        It's true   I was born lucky

found my heart floating   down river   caught in tendrils   of wild rice
    traded my gently used words   to a Cave Salamander   who told me I couldn't

keep mapping stories   if they weren't my own   he flicked my tuning fork bones
      & told me   other people needed   to sing my pitch

A BEDTIME STORY ABOUT
THE HEART

The only thing sensible about the heart is its shoes.
    When the heart is sent away from home
        it only takes a small brown suitcase filled with air—

the reason is unclear, but like I said, the only thing sensible
    about the heart is its little white sneakers. Every heart starts
        out like this—with pristine shoes that stay that way until

it's sent out into the world. The heart is accustomed to being carried.
    Every heart is sent away from the body eventually
        to live with a new person for a while. Just to check things out.

The new person learns that the heart melts a little
    when it's given coffee in the morning & how it likes its
        fruit to be cut instead of eating it whole & that it swallows

pomegranate seeds & that it can't sing in key.
    This heart has no rhythm.
        Or the heart's needs are neglected & it rubs its shoes in the dirt

waiting for promises to be fulfilled. Some hearts are twisted
    for the fun of it. Some are left blindfolded in the trunk
        of an Oldsmobile somewhere in Nevada.

If the person the heart stays with is good & kind,
    the heart will send a telegram home & ask its body to come join them.
        But if that's not the case, then the heart must walk back home.

It trips & falls a lot since hearts are top heavy. Its little shoes
get covered in brown dust & fill with water when it rains.
The heart gets lost a lot on the way back because it doesn't know how

to ask for directions or receive help. Eventually the heart makes it
home, a bit bruised—sometimes a little worse for wear or addled.
But I've never heard of a heart that didn't make it back.

If the heart makes this trip enough times, it'll trade up for black boots.
But not always. Sometimes the heart wears the soles off its sneakers,
lets the white stay brown & puts duct tape over the holes.

I want to tell you all hearts find good homes eventually.
I want to tell you they're all taken care of forever.
I want to tell you that the body treats the heart well

when it comes home after its long journey. But the truth is,
the heart's body inflicts wounds worse than any other person could.
So I hope someday I find my heart's boots abandoned at a roadside

museum full of dinosaur bones. The heart's suitcase left butterflied in a small town.

I hope when I call its name, it never answers.

ENDING IN CONTRITION OR RESIGNATION

I was never in love with a city
                & woke new,
light as moth dust
                   every few months.

I wandered each watercolor metropolis
                until its streets cooed my name,
harmonizing
              under my feet.

The very next day I would leave
            another white bed wrinkled,
still cradling a lover, at times,
             reaching out a dove's wing in their sleep.

On every coast, I've taken lovers
to witness local miracles. Wonder is all I have
           to gift before

I continue outrunning
           my gold-leafed memory.
Its silhouette casting rose
           shadows on the pavement
behind me, but nowhere else.

Forgive me, restlessness, I have sinned.
　　　It has been [   ] months
since my last confession.

I confess:
　　　　　　I cried on a train crossing the Hudson
　　　　once, wanting so badly to live
　　　as particles in the ginger light.

I confess:

　　I woke up last night sure
　　　　　my arms vined around my beloved,
　　river steady breathing
　　　　　rippling from his body.

A few minutes dissolved
　　before I had enough courage
to search the blankets & find what I already knew—

that I held nothing.

　　　　　　| Here is where contrition should be recited but won't be |
| Here is where I listen for butterfly wings
　　　　& know it's my beloved sighing in his sleep |

Dear restlessness,
Dear desire to disintegrate,

　　I give you up.

WHEN JOY SPLIT OPEN

the moon inched closer,
    howling like a harmonica.
you held a mountain
    plucked from ivory
between your teeth.
    my fingertips each ran
through agave fields
    along your body until dawn
rose blushing at the skyline.
    joy split open at its seams
& seeds fell out. I measure
    distance in stellar magnitude—
how smallness becomes larger
    when held closer.

SEEDS

All morning I daydreamed while watching
the chickens spinning gold in the yard.
Just before you arrived, I ransacked the gray sky
pocketing my tender thoughts & handed you
the key over the tall gate, not knowing if
you're letting me out or I'm letting you in.
I glance over while cutting the pear you
brought me & see you in soft focus, writing—
the engine of your mind singing in minor key.

A song that isn't meant for me but I eavesdrop.
After all day quietly memorizing what I like
most. I only tell you, *You're nothing without that
dimple when you smile.* Which you think is funny
& I squirm knowing the words I meant to say
have gotten lost on their way & taken up camp
in my heart. Last night I worried you'd want
more than I could give. But you didn't & you don't
& my lips are swollen petals & your mouth
tastes sweet of coconut milk, five spice, & ginger.
I fall asleep & wake up sleep-hazed
in your arms thinking,

> *Does what grows inside me,*
> *grow inside you too?*

BOILING PUFFINS

or were they penguins? 3 million
boiled into lamp oil
        & their beaks sold
as children's masks during summer festivals.

Listen, I don't know if the last part is true.
My mind adds extra details to every story.

Like when my dad buys kitchen knives
at garage sales, it feels ominous.
He says, *No one can ever have enough good knives.*

I'm sure people sell used kitchen knives all the time.
    Serrated blades are a hot seller, amiright?

But the year we got a dog,
my dad's coworker stabbed his wife
until she played dead

& the cops never found that knife,
so I worry about the history of everyday objects.

I shop at Target since *vintage* & *antique*
are ways of saying *pre-haunted.*

I get the heebie jeebies easy. I have goose bumps
thinking about the smell of antique promise rings.

Listen, I shouldn't be hypocritical. I've told all my lovers
that my body is full of ghosts,
                              but who hasn't, right?

I've told them to please not touch
the scar on my thigh.
                    It's from a hunting knife.

I've told them antique shop rules apply:
You Break, You Buy.

When I'm driving, I wonder about cars & dogs
left on the roadside.
            Especially those near rivers & lakes,
would I ever leave mine abandoned like that?

I read once that over half a million people disappear
every year in the U.S.
                      & there's not enough milk cartons
for all their faces because of millennials
    who've ruined the milk & cereal industry.

I've heard the mind forgets trauma
if it loves its owner enough.

But, listen, that one probably isn't true
            I read it on a message board in 2006.

When I can't sleep, I read wikiHows
about erasing myself from the internet.
It's easier than you would think

to leave & never be found. It's easier
to start new, as someone else sometimes.

If someday my car is found abandoned by the river,

my cell phone vibrating in the knife drawer,

would you listen for me late at night
putting my key in the door?

Would you believe me if I told you I left
something important at home & came back,
put my head on your chest & just listened?

8 CHICKENS IN A PAPIER-MÂCHÉ HUMAN: A BEDTIME STORY

imagine if it was steam powered,
the brass endoskeleton heaving.

angled movements, rigid. 16 taloned feet
pulling levers in tight precision.

roiling clouds & feathers
peaking through uneven paper layers,

steam warping the paper inside out. imagine
the papier-mâché human lays awake at night,

white light of a billion stars rushing
through the window blinds. each chicken nested

in a secret bunker below the floorboards,
softly cawing in their feathered sleep.

the papier-mâché human continues smiling,
never blinking in the moonlight of absence.

perhaps thinking

about the human family sleeping in the other wall boxes.
wondering if they dream about being made

into paper cranes like he would if he could dream.
curious why a big box full of smaller boxes

is called a "house" & if longing can be solved
by folding it small enough to fit in a pocket.

outside the coyotes sharpen their knives
on each other's whetstone teeth.

like all good squatters, they write field notes
& watch until the day they massacre a lineage.

imagine the smallest human in the family
wrestling tumbleweeds in the dust every day

while the chickens inside the papier-mâché human
eat corn nuts in the shed, building a rocket

to take them away from earth. they've learned
to make fuel from grinding their eggshells.

every sacrifice is a promise for better.
the papier-mâché human knows

these plans don't include him.
he knows the chickens will leave

his body in a fleshy heap or perhaps ripped
into confetti to celebrate their success.

his brass endoskeleton will be used for parts or discarded
in the desert with all the other skeletons.

a gathering of tumbleweeds is called a departure
but sometimes the smallest human thinks it's called a wish.

someday the small one knows the coyotes will come
with knives in their mouths & steal his good avocado

growing land for themselves. not even the tumbleweeds
will protect him. he worries about future feudalism.

he worries he'll grow up to be like his Pop
or a vanishing point on every skyline.

he worries more about this than the coyotes
& begins humming a song. he once heard

the body's acoustics
can convince all good things to stay,

can make time spin around
in the same moment for eternity.

but it isn't true. the smallest human hums
& the rumbling of the chickens' rocket muffles

his vibrations. the coyotes use this opportunity
to attack but can't stop coughing when they smell burnt eggshells.

the departure of tumbleweeds gets blown away
by the rocket's thrusters & the papier-mâché human

flies for the first time, imagining himself a paper crane,
into a nearby loquat tree. still smiling, his arm sways as if waving.

imagine the small human wasn't mistaken—
that a departure is actually a wish.

BEFORE YOU VISITED

I lock-boxed every 50-cent piece
of vending machine jewelry

still inside their acorn capsules,
each one, a childhood prophecy.

I scattered holy water & salt-
ed the boiling pan until it turned ocean.

Vacuumed the bird's nest
inside the fireplace,
still full of fox fur

nebula-colored eggs
cracked like bone

china, gold filling the crevices.
I've always filled time this way.

But I left the front door open
& cats gathered on the lawn.

They left koi on the porch in piles
& hid mice in the flowerpots.

I would have flooded the street
in candlelight had I known
you'd be here so soon.

I would have hidden
my fists in my pockets,
until compressed diamonds.

I would have traded
diamonds for starlight.

I would have made the world
give itself up to you. I would have

welcomed you to never leave.

ACKNOWLEDGMENTS

Thank you to the editors of the following publications where these poems first appeared:

The Acentos Review: "The Long Trajectory of Grief"

AGNI: "Mother // Monster"

Black Warrior Review: "8 Chickens in a Papier-Mâché Human: A Bedtime Story"

The Boiler: "If I Invited You to Love Me"

Breakwater Review: "Inside the Foxhole"

Cosmonauts Avenue: "Sardine Spine"

Cream City Review: "Uncertainty with Fish Scales"

Drunken Boat: "Trapping Season"

Grist: A Journal of the Literary Arts: "Down by the Water," "Ending in Contrition or Resignation," & "Solar Eclipse // Myself in Orbit"

Palette Poetry: "Baby Teeth"

PANK: "Before You Visited"

Puerto del Sol: "Before Skipping Town"

Radar Poetry: "Crush," "Heart Attack," "Home Is Where the Closet Is," & "Girl's Guide to Leaving"

Redivider: "When Joy Split Open" & "A Bedtime Story about the Heart"

Reservoir: "(My)thology"

Sakura Review: "I Still Check for Monsters before I Go to Bed"

Stirring: A Literary Collection: "Slash and Burn"

Syzygy: "The Astronomer's Daughter"

Vinyl: "Curas & Dichos"

Waxwing Magazine: "Boiling Puffins"

Zócalo Public Square: "Thanksgivings"

Thank you to the folks at the University of Wisconsin Press & Wisconsin Poetry Series editors Sean Bishop & Ron Wallace & the series readers.

Thank you, Carmen Giménez Smith.

My immense gratitude to the Stadler Center for Poetry & Literary Arts. Thank you, Chet'la Sebree, Andrew Ciotola, & Joe Scapellato for the gift of time. It has provided the space for me to revise, think, & shape these pages. I can't imagine this book without you all.

A great deal of gratitude for my teachers & workshop leaders: Rigoberto González, Willie Perdomo, Danez Smith, A. Van Jordan, & Brenda Shaughnessy. I carry your lessons with me as I write & edit.

Thank you to Melissa Hartland & my MFA cohort.

Thank you: Tina Zafreen Alam, Emilie Collins, Michelle Hart, Mel & Audrie King, Muriel Leung, Nathan Moore, Christopher Morgan, Christina Ortiz, V. Ruiz, Ben Seanor, Bob Sykora, Olvard Liche Smith, Laura Spence-Ash, & Michelle Trujillo.

Forever & ever in awe of my VONA beloveds—how fortunate I've been to witness y'all shine: Jubi Arriola-Headley, Ana Portnoy Brimmer, Malcolm Friend, April Gibson, JR Mahung, Mark Maza, Nuri Nusrat, & Brittany Rogers.

T. K. Lê, thank you for holding space for my writing every April. So many of these poems started in 30/30. Thank you to all the 30/30 writers who have written alongside me.

To my family: all my love & gratitude. Thank you for believing I could do this.

Alfredo Aguilar, my partner in all things, thank you for holding these poems & book in all their stages.

And thank you, dear reader.

WISCONSIN POETRY SERIES

Edited by Ronald Wallace and Sean Bishop

(B) = Winner of the Brittingham Prize in Poetry
(FP) = Winner of the Felix Pollak Prize in Poetry
(4L) = Winner of the Four Lakes Prize in Poetry

Immortality (4L) • Alan Feldman

A Sail to Great Island (FP) • Alan Feldman

The Word We Used for It (B) • Max Garland

A Field Guide to the Heavens (B) • Frank X. Gaspar

The Royal Baker's Daughter (FP) • Barbara Goldberg

Fractures (FP) • Carlos Andrés Gómez

Gloss • Rebecca Hazelton

Funny (FP) • Jennifer Michael Hecht

Queen in Blue • Ambalila Hemsell

The Legend of Light (FP) • Bob Hicok

Sweet Ruin (B) • Tony Hoagland

Partially Excited States (FP) • Charles Hood

Ripe (FP) • Roy Jacobstein

Perigee (B) • Diane Kerr

American Parables (B) • Daniel Khalastchi

Saving the Young Men of Vienna (B) • David Kirby

Conditions of the Wounded • Anna Leigh Knowles

Ganbatte (FP) • Sarah Kortemeier

Falling Brick Kills Local Man (FP) • Mark Kraushaar

Last Seen (FP) • Jacqueline Jones LaMon

The Lightning That Strikes the Neighbors' House (FP) • Nick Lantz

You, Beast (B) • Nick Lantz

The Explosive Expert's Wife • Shara Lessley

The Unbeliever (B) • Lisa Lewis

Slow Joy (B) • Stephanie Marlis

Acts of Contortion (B) • Anna George Meek

Blood Aria • Christopher Nelson

Come Clean (FP) • Joshua Nguyen

Bardo (B) • Suzanne Paola

Meditations on Rising and Falling (B) • Philip Pardi

Old and New Testaments (B) • Lynn Powell

Season of the Second Thought (FP) • Lynn Powell

A Path between Houses (B) • Greg Rappleye

The Book of Hulga (FP) • Rita Mae Reese

Why Can't It Be Tenderness (FP) • Michelle Brittan Rosado

Don't Explain (FP) • Betsy Sholl

House of Sparrows: New and Selected Poems (4L) • Betsy Sholl